D0206977

Chinese Water Dragons (Physignathus Cocincinus) As Pets

By Auric Smith

Chinese Water Dragons/Lizards Care, Care Sheet,
Habitat, Cages, Enclosure, Diet, Tanks, Facts, Set Up,
Food, Names, Pictures, Info, Shedding, Life Span,
Breeding, Feeding, Cost All Included.

Chinese Water Dragons

A Complete Owner's Guide

**Including Chinese Water Dragons Care Sheet,
Facts and Information**

Copyright © 2013 All Rights Reserved

Copyright and Trademarks

This publication is copyright 2013 by IGNL Publishing. All rights reserved. Reproduction or redistribution of this publication, in part or in whole, is expressly prohibited without the permission of the publisher. This includes scanning or photocopying (except for personal use), storing the document in a retrieval system, producing electronic copies or distributing the document, in whole or in part, without permission.

Disclaimer and Legal Notice

This product is not legal or accounting advice and should not be interpreted in that manner. You need to do your own due-diligence to determine if the content of this product is right for your animal. The author of this product is not liable for any damages or losses associated with the content in this product. While every attempt has been made to verify the information shared in this publication, however the author does not assume any responsibility for errors, omissions or contrary interpretation of the subject matter herein. Any perceived slights to any specific person(s) or organization(s) are purely unintentional.

We have no control over the nature, content and availability of the web sites listed in this book. The inclusion of any web site links does not necessarily imply a recommendation or endorse the views expressed within them. IGNL Publishing takes no responsibility for, and will not be liable for, the websites being temporarily unavailable or being removed from the internet.

The accuracy and completeness of information provided herein and opinions stated herein are not guaranteed or warranted to produce any particular results, and the advice and strategies, contained herein may not suitable for every individual. The author should not be liable for any loss incurred as a consequence of the use and application, directly or indirectly, information in regards to the subject matter covered.

A catalogue record of this book is available at the British Library

Foreword

In this book you will find all of the information you need to care for your Chinese Water Dragons. Included in this book is information about Chinese Water Dragon care, care sheet, habitat, cages, enclosure, diet, tanks, facts, set up, food, names, pictures, info, shedding, life span, breeding, feeding and cost. After reading this book you will be an expert on the Chinese Water Dragon!

Acknowledgements

I would like to thank my two beautiful children Alexander and Sam for providing the inspiration to write this book. After begging me to get a Chinese Water Dragon for months on end I finally agreed and it was one of the best choices I have ever made.

I would also like to thank my wife Tricia for supporting me throughout this wonderful journey.

Table of Contents

Chapter One: Introduction

The name "Chinese Water Dragon" might inspire images of a spiked reptile of mythical size but that is not the case. Chinese Water Dragons are actually very friendly reptiles which makes them excellent pets. These creatures typically grow up to 3 feet (1 meter) long and they can be a joy to keep as a family pet. In this book you will learn the basics about what these lizards are, where they come from and how they came to be popular as pets. You will also learn where and how to purchase these reptiles and what is required to keep them safe and healthy.

If you have ever wanted a unique and wonderful pet, consider the Chinese Water Dragon. These reptiles are like no other pet you have ever had. In addition to being unique in appearance, these reptiles are also unique in being very friendly with their human caretakers. Chinese Water Dragons are much friendlier than iguanas and they are a better choice for families with children. These lizards do require a certain amount of care, so before you make the decision to purchase one you should carefully read this book to make sure you give your dragon the best care.

Chapter Two: Understanding Chinese Water Dragons

1.) What Are Chinese Water Dragons?

Chinese Water Dragons are known by the scientific name *Physignatus cocincinus* and they belong to the family Agamidae. These lizards are native to East and Southeast Asia and they belong to the same group as bearded dragons and uromastyx. The Chinese Water Dragon is known by a number of alternate names including Asian Water Dragon, Green Water Dragon and Thai Water Dragon. These lizards can be found throughout the lowland and highland forests of China, India and other countries in Southeast Asia.

Chinese Water Dragons belong to the Physignathus genus in the family Agamidae. The Physignathus genus contains only two species, the Chinese Water Dragon and the Australian Water Dragon (*Physignathus lesueurii*). Whereas the Chinese Water Dragon is found throughout Southeastern Asia, the Australian Water Dragon is only found in Australia where it is locally known as the Eastern Water Dragon.

The Chinese Water Dragon is a large green lizard that tends to favor semi-aquatic freshwater environments. In the wild, these lizards can most often be found along the banks of freshwater lakes and freshwater streams. These reptiles are diurnal which means they are most active during the day. These lizards spend the majority of their day in the trees and, if they feel threatened, they will drop from the tree into the water and swim to safety. Chinese Water Dragons can stay submerged for up to 25 minutes and they are very capable swimmers.

2.) Facts About Chinese Water Dragons

Chinese Water Dragons can reach a length of up to 1 meter (3 feet) at maturity, measured from head to tail. Females of the species may only grow to about 2 feet in length while males tend to grow larger. These lizards generally exhibit green coloration, though it may range from light to dark green and may be accompanied by diagonal stripes running the length of the body.

The tail of Chinese Water Dragons typically exhibits green or dark brown bands that start in the middle of the tail and extend toward the tip. The undersides of these lizards are typically white, pale green or pale yellow. One of the most attractive features of these lizards is their colorful throats. Some dragons exhibit yellow or orange coloration on the throat and some display a striped pattern.

About 70% of these lizards' length is made up of the tail. The tails of these lizards are somewhat flat and tapered from the base to a fine point at the tip. A Chinese Water Dragon uses its tail for balance and leverage in climbing – it can also be used to whip predators if the dragon is feeling threatened. The tail also plays a role in swimming.

Chinese Water Dragons have triangular-shaped heads and the heads of male dragons are larger than those of females. Adult male dragons also develop large crests on the head, neck and tail. Female dragons have similar crests but they are not as large as they are in the male. Males of the species may also display more vivid coloring than female dragons.

Chinese Water Dragons have strong legs for climbing and swimming. Their front legs are slender, having five toes to help them with climbing and grasping branches. The hind legs are muscular, used for both jumping and climbing, though they are also helpful in swimming. On the back feet, the middle of the five toes is longest and all claws end in needle-like points.

Like many other reptiles, Chinese Water Dragons have an iridescent photosensitive spot between their eyes. This spot is called a pineal gland (or third eye) and it plays a role in thermoregulating the dragon's body by sensing differences in light. The tongue of these lizards is sticky which helps them to catch and hold prey – the teeth of these lizards are small and pointed.

Chinese Water Dragons are generally friendly – in fact, they are considered much friendlier than other pet lizards such as iguanas. To prevent these lizards from becoming aggressive, regular handling is recommended. These lizards have an average lifespan between 10 and 15 years, those they can live as long as 20 years if properly cared for.

Summary of Chinese Water Dragon Facts

Scientific Name: *Physignatus cocincinus*
Habitat: East and Southeast Asia
Size: up to 3 feet (females average 2 feet)
Coloration: light to dark green; banding on tail; bright color on throat; light on underside
Build: tail composes 70% of body length; legs are muscular for climbing and swimming; 5 toes with sharp claws; head is triangular in shape; crest or horns on head, neck and tail

Temperament: friendly; requires regular handling to prevent aggressive behavior

Lifespan: average 10 to 15 years, can reach 20 years

Diet: omnivorous, prefers insects and whole prey over fruits and vegetables

3.) Wild vs. Captive Chinese Water Dragons

Chinese Water Dragons are very popular as exotic pets and you can find dragons that are wild-caught as well as those that are captive-bred. Before purchasing one of these reptiles, it would be wise to learn the difference between the two so you can choose which option is best for you. You should also take the precaution of asking the associates at your local pet store whether the dragons they are selling are captive-bred or wild-caught.

Wild-caught Chinese Water Dragons are more likely to carry disease, particularly parasites. If you introduce a wild dragon into a cage with captive-bred dragons, you may have problems with the spread of parasites or other diseases. Dragons taken from the wild may also be experiencing a great deal of stress, having been removed from their natural habitat and put through the shipping process. It has also been said that wild-caught dragons have a less even temperament than those that have been captive-bred.

If you want a Chinese Water Dragon that is friendly and playful, your best bet is to buy one that has been captive-bred. Captive-bred lizards are more adaptable to life in a cage and they are more likely to respond well to handling by their owners. Wild-caught dragons have a tendency to bite or tail whip, particularly when they are feeling threatened.

4.) Types of Chinese Water Dragons

There is only one species of Chinese Water Dragon, but there are other similar lizard species. The closest genetic relative to the Chinese Water Dragon is the Australian Water Dragon (*Physignathus lesueurii*). These lizards are native to Eastern Australia and are also known by the names Eastern Water Dragon and Gippsland Water Dragon.

Australian Water Dragons typically achieve a maximum length around 3 feet (2 feet for females) and their tails comprise almost 2/3 of their total length. These lizards have powerful legs and a spiked crest running own the length of the spine. Australian Water Dragons are typically olive or brown in color with banding along the body and across the chest. These lizards can be kept as pets, but Chinese Water Dragons are more popular.

5.) Chinese Water Dragons vs. Bearded Dragons

Although these two lizards have names that sound alike, Chinese Water Dragons are very different from Bearded Dragons. One major difference between these two animals is their size – Bearded Dragons typically reach a maximum length between 16 and 20 inches (40 – 51cm) while mature Chinese Water Dragons can grow to over 3 feet long. This translates to very different habitat requirements. Bearded Dragons require a tank between 40 and 55 gallons (150 to 208 liters) in capacity while 75 gallons (284 liters) is considered the minimum for Chinese Water Dragons.

There are also a number of differences in terms of habitat between these two lizards. Bearded Dragons are naturally found in a very arid environment while Chinese Water

Dragons come from a humid, semi-aquatic environment. Bearded Dragons do require access to fresh water, but only for drinking purposes, whereas Chinese Water Dragons like to swim and soak in water on a regular basis. Chinese Water Dragons also differ from Bearded Dragons in that they like to climb and thus require a tank that provides height as well as depth.

Bearded dragons are more adaptable to cooler temperatures than Chinese Water Dragons, but they do still require basking areas. Proper basking area temperature for Bearded Dragons ranges from 85° to 95°F (29° - 35°C) while the rest of the cage can be kept between 68° and 77°F (20° - 25°C). Chinese Water Dragons, on the other hand, require a minimum temperature between 75° and 80°F (24° - 27°C) with a basking temperature around 90°F (32°C). Chinese Water Dragons also require a more humid environment than Bearded Dragons.

Chinese Water Dragons and Bearded Dragons follow a similar diet – both lizards are omnivorous and both can accept live prey. Bearded Dragons subsist mainly on crickets, worms and leafy greens while Chinese Water Dragons may require more live prey. Chinese Water Dragons only eat every two to three days while Bearded Dragons should be fed once a day or every other day.

Chinese Water Dragons are friendly animals by nature, but they can become aggressive when two males are kept together. Chinese Water Dragons are best kept in groups or pairs, but Bearded Dragons can be kept individually. Unlike

Chinese Water Dragons, Bearded Dragons are non-aggressive and can be kept in any combination of the two sexes provide there is enough space to accommodate them.

6.) Chinese Water Dragons vs. Iguanas

Though Chinese Water Dragons and Iguanas look very similar as juveniles, they grow to be two very different reptiles. Whereas Chinese Water Dragons are known for being friendly as pets, Iguanas have a tendency to become testy and their sharp claws can do serious damage. Iguanas are also more likely to bite than Chinese Water Dragons and a bite from an iguana can be very dangerous, transmitting bacteria and resulting in permanent scarring.

Another significant difference between these two lizards is their size. Chinese Water Dragons typically grow to about 2 feet for females and 3 feet for males – adult iguanas, on the other hand, typically grow to a minimum of 4 feet in length and can grow as long as 6 feet if properly cared for. Due to their large size, iguanas require a great deal more space than Chinese Water Dragons but both lizards enjoy having things to climb on in their enclosure.

Iguanas come from a very hot and arid environment, so an iguana cage should be maintained at a temperature between 85° and 95°F (29° - 35°C) with basking areas in the temperature range of 110° to 115°F (43° - 46°C). Temperatures at night should not drop below 70°F (21°C). These temperatures are slightly higher than those required by Chinese Water Dragons with the exception of the basking area temperature which is significantly higher for iguanas.

The diet of these two lizards is very different. Though vegetables and fruits comprise part of a Chinese Water Dragon's diet, these foods are the sole source of nutrition for iguanas. Iguanas should never be offered animal proteins whereas Chinese Water Dragons regularly feed on live prey. An iguana's diet should be comprised of a wide variety of leafy greens, fruits, and other vegetables.

When making the choice between an iguana and a Chinese Water Dragon, it is largely a matter of preference. Both lizards require a great deal of commitment in terms of time and resources but iguanas require more space and a more specialized diet. Iguanas are also less friendly than Chinese Water Dragons and may not be a good choice for children.

Chapter Three: What to Know Before You Buy

1.) Do You Need a License?

All reptiles require a special permit and most species are protected by federal law against removing them from the wild. This is generally not an issue for U.S. and U.K. residents because Chinese Water Dragons are not native to these areas. You will, however, need to obtain a permit in order to keep a captive-bred Chinese Water Dragon as a pet. Licensing requirements may be different in the U.S. than they are in the U.K. and Australia.

a.) U.S. Licensing Requirements

The US Fish and Wildlife Service is responsible for regulating the trade and keeping of live animals in the United States. Federal laws regulating the sale or keeping of reptiles only apply to species that are native to the U.S. and to species that are considered threatened or endangered. Chinese Water Dragons are not native to the United States nor are they listed as an endangered species by the Endangered Species Act.

In terms of state regulations, licensing for keeping reptiles may vary by state. In most cases, however, there are no licensing requirements for Chinese Water Dragons. About half of all states in the U.S. have no regulations restricting the importation or keeping of nonnative reptiles but some states require a permit to import any live wildlife. Other states only require permits for venomous or dangerous reptiles and amphibians. To determine whether your state requires a permit for keeping Chinese Water Dragons, contact your state office.

Some states which may require a license for nonnative reptiles include:

Colorado

Florida

Delaware

Maine

Massachusetts

Nevada

New Jersey	Tennessee
Rhode Island	Virginia

b.) U.K. Licensing Requirements

Federal regulations in the U.K. generally do not require a permit for the keeping of pet reptiles or amphibians as long as they are not dangerous. The Dangerous Wild Animals Act of 1976 prohibits the keeping of certain species without a license. Some of the species included in this list are: crocodiles, alligators, caimans, asps, cobras and other venomous snakes. Chinese Water Dragons are not included in the list of dangerous species. To be completely sure you do not need a permit to keep one of these reptiles, contact your local council.

c.) Australian Licensing Requirements

In order to legally keep a Chinese Water Dragon as a pet, you may need to obtain a license from the Office of Environment and Heritage (OEH). There are two different classes of license for keeping reptiles. A Class 1 license authorizes an individual to keep some of the most common species of reptiles – this is the type of license you will need for a Chinese Water Dragon. A Class 2 license is for those who plan to keep rare or difficult species. Australian Licensing requirements typically apply to native or endangered species only, but it would be wise to check with your local council to be absolutely sure you do not need a permit to keep a Chinese Water Dragon.

In order to obtain a Class 1 license, you must be at least 16 years old or have the application submitted by a parent or legal guardian. After obtaining a license yourself, you should be sure to purchase your Chinese Water Dragons from a suitably licensed pet shop or a licensed breeder. If you are importing the animal from another state, you may also need to apply for an interstate import license.

2.) How Many Should You Buy?

Chinese Water Dragons can be kept on their own, but they tend to do better in groups. These lizards can be very social and, in the right circumstances, they can be downright friendly. If you do plan to buy more than one Chinese Water Dragon, be sure not to purchase more than one male unless you have multiple cages. You can, however, keep two or three females together in one cage if you do not plan to breed your dragons.

A single male dragon can be kept with two or three females, provided the cage is large enough to accommodate them. In the wild, Chinese Water Dragons typically live in groups consisting of one male and several females. The male is often very dominant and territorial, fighting off other males that enter his territory. Keeping two or three dragons is not significantly more work than a single dragon and your dragons will be happier in groups.

3.) Can They be Kept with Other Pets?

It is possible to keep Chinese Water Dragons in the same enclosure as other reptiles, but you should use extreme caution in doing so. You first need to ensure that both reptile species have similar habitat requirements and that neither will grow to be significantly larger than the other. In decorating the enclosure, you need to provide plenty of basking areas so the two species have places to hide and to establish as their "territory".

It is never a good idea to keep Chinese Water Dragons with iguanas because iguanas grow up to 7 feet long and they can be very aggressive. You should also avoid keeping your

Chinese Water Dragon with geckos or bearded dragons. These lizards have very different habitat requirements and they are not likely to get along with Chinese Water Dragons. Combining these species in the same space is likely to result in injury or death to one or more of your lizards.

Keeping Chinese Water Dragons in a home with other pets can also be tricky. Your first concern should be preventing other pets from accessing your dragon's enclosure. The enclosure should be topped with a tight-fitting lid and it should be kept in an area that other pets cannot reach. Even if you prevent other pets from getting into your dragon's enclosure, their presence can cause your dragon to become stressed.

Chinese Water Dragons can be shy at times and may be alarmed by loud noises or the presence of other animals near their cage. If you absolutely must keep your dragons along with other pets, be very careful and be sure to supervise any time your pets spend together in the same space, inside or outside the enclosure.

4.) Ease and Cost of Care

Chinese Water Dragons are fairly easy to keep and you do not require a great deal of experience or expertise with reptiles in order to keep them. The main concern with these lizards is that they require a great deal of space and a varied diet in order to remain healthy. As long as you are able to provide these things, however, you should have little difficulty keeping these lizards.

The cost of keeping Chinese Water Dragons will vary depending on the number of dragons you keep and the complexity of your enclosure. You will also have to factor in the cost of Chinese Water Dragon supplies. Keep in mind that a 75-gallon (284 liters) tank is the recommended minimum for these lizards – this could cost you $200 (£133) for a simple glass tank. Specialized or custom-built enclosures can become very expensive. You also need to factor in the cost for decorating the tank with live plants, basking sites and water areas.

Purchasing a Chinese Water Dragon should only cost you $20 to $50 (£13 - £33) depending where you buy. If you plan to keep multiple dragons, you will need to multiply this figure accordingly which could result in a significant cost. Add to that the cost of feeding multiple dragons and you could be looking at a significant financial investment. Adult dragons only eat a few times per week, but you will need to keep multiple types of food on hand in addition to calcium supplements.

Not only do you need to pay for the initial set-up of your Chinese Water Dragon cage, but you also have to think about maintenance costs. You will need to initially invest in heating and lighting equipment, and then you will need to pay the cost of keeping that equipment running on a monthly basis. Again, these costs will depend on the size of your enclosure and the number of dragons you intend to keep.

a.) Summary of Costs

Dragon Purchase: $20 to $50 each (£13 - £33)
Enclosure: $150-$300 for a glass tank; specialized or custom-built enclosures may be more costly (£100 - £200)
Equipment: lighting and heating ($20 to $50; £13 - £33)
Decorations: live plants, basking sites, water areas ($30 to $100; £20 - £67)
Food: regular supply of multiple feeder insects, fruits or veggies, calcium supplements (insects $3 to $5, produce $5 to $10, calcium $10) (£2 - £3.5; £3.5; £7)
Other Costs and Supplies: routine veterinary care, cage upkeep and repairs, replacement bulbs, etc. ($20 to $100; £13 - £67)

b.) Breakdown of Monthly Costs

Live Food: $20 to $30 (£13 - £20)
Fresh Produce: $15 to $25 (£10 - £17)
Calcium Supplements: $10 (£7)
Replacement Bulbs: $10 (£7)
Utilities: $10 - $20 (£7– £13)
Replacement Plants: $10 (£7)

**Note: Prices may vary due to currency fluctuation.

5.) Pros and Cons of Chinese Water Dragons

As is true of any pet, Chinese Water Dragons have their pros and cons. Before you purchase one of these lizards it would be wise to familiarize yourself with both the pros and cons. That way, you will be able to make an informed decision as to whether a Chinese Water Dragon is the right pet for you.

Pros of Chinese Water Dragons

- Relatively easy to care for
- Adults only need to be fed 3 times per week
- Very friendly if properly socialized
- Lizards themselves are not terribly expensive to buy
- Can be very entertaining pets
- Dietary supplementation is generally not needed if given a well-balanced diet
- Very attractive lizards, beautiful colors
- Generally very tame, easy to handle (not aggressive)

Cons of Chinese Water Dragons

- Can grow very large (up to 3 feet)

- Require very large enclosures (at least 75 gallons; 284 liters)
- Specific dietary needs – can be picky eaters
- Often urinate/defecate in water – requires regular refreshing and sanitizing of water pans
- Requires vertical space as well as horizontal space to accommodate climbing needs
- Initial costs for building/stocking enclosure can be very high
- High humidity levels required in enclosure

Chapter Four: Life Stages of Chinese Water Dragons

Baby Chinese Water Dragon

Though Chinese Water Dragons grow fairly large in adulthood, baby dragons only measure about five inches (13 cm) from nose to tail. The coloring of baby dragons is slightly different from that of adults – many baby dragons are often brown or pale green in color with light stripes on the body. While they are still babies, these reptiles should be fed small meals on a daily basis. The best foods for baby Chinese Water Dragons are small crickets and wax worms.

Juvenile Chinese Water Dragon

As baby Chinese Water Dragons grow, they will be able to accept larger foods. Juvenile Chinese Water Dragons can eat larger crickets, wax worms, silkworms and other insects. Because they are still growing, juvenile dragons should be fed every day. It is also a good idea to dust their food every other day with powdered calcium.

Full Grown Chinese Water Dragon

Chinese Water Dragons typically reach their full length between 18 and 24 months. For females, a full grown Chinese Water Dragon will measure around 2 feet in length while a male will be closer to 3 feet in length. Once they are past the juvenile stage, you only need to feed your dragons every two or three days. Though Chinese Water Dragons are omnivorous by nature, they tend to prefer insects so it is best to offer them a variety of live prey.

Female Chinese Water Dragon

Female Chinese Water Dragons only grow to about 2 feet in length -- they may also be less colorful than males of the species. Female dragons also have slightly smaller heads, crests and spikes than males. Keeping a female Chinese Water Dragon requires a little extra care because she will lay eggs on a regular basis, regardless whether they have been fertilized or not. In order to keep your female dragon healthy, you need to make sure to feed her a well-balanced diet.

Maintaining a proper temperature in the tank is also very important, especially when the dragon is pregnant. While your female Chinese Water Dragon is pregnant, you should also plan to supplement her diet with calcium on a daily basis to ensure that the eggs develop properly. You will also need to provide your dragon with a place to lay her eggs. This area should be filled to a depth of 8 to 10 inches (20 to 25 cm) with soil or peat moss kept slightly damp. Your dragon will dig into the soil to prepare a place to lay her eggs.

Adult Male Chinese Water Dragon

Adult Chinese Water Dragons exhibit slightly different coloration than juveniles of the species. An adult dragon will be light or dark green in color with some darker banding along the tail. Adult male dragons develop larger, wider heads than females and the spikes running down their back are generally longer. Male dragons also have a more triangular shape overall, compared to a female dragon's more rounded shape.

Senior Chinese Water Dragons

After a certain age, Chinese Water Dragons stop exhibiting signs of growth. In their own age, they may also become less active and might eat less as well. As female dragons age, they may begin laying eggs less frequently.

Chapter Five: Purchasing Chinese Water Dragons

1.) Where to Buy Chinese Water Dragons

There are a number of places you can find Chinese Water Dragons for sale in both the U.S. and the U.K. Because the sale of these lizards generally doesn't require a license, you can buy them from your local pet store, from individual breeders, or from online advertisements. Before you buy a Chinese Water Dragon you need to not only be sure it is the right pet for you, but you should also be sure the source you are purchasing from is responsible.

Check your local pet store to see if they have Chinese Water Dragons available or if they plan to have them in the future.

These lizards are sometimes a seasonal pet, only available after the hibernation/breeding season. Another option is to contact the herpetological society in your area to find local breeders. Before choosing a breeder, take the time to contact several different people and ask questions to ascertain the individual's experience with and knowledge of these lizards. If you buy from a breeder who doesn't know much about Chinese Water Dragons, the chances are good that the dragon you buy won't be completely healthy or well-bred.

You also need to be careful in purchasing reptiles from pet stores. Some pet stores sell wild-caught dragons which can be more difficult than captive-bred specimens to care for. Take the time to ask questions at your local pet store to find out where the dragons were obtained from and what kind of condition they are in.

Note: Purchasing animals online is not the best option because shipping live animals is cruel. It is difficult to control the temperatures and conditions to which the animals are exposed and transport companies may not exercise the proper care in handling the animals. I encourage you to purchase your Chinese Water Dragons from a pet store or a breeder rather than ordering them online.

2.) How to Select a Healthy Specimen

In addition to making sure that you purchase your Chinese Water Dragons from a reputable source, you should also be sure that the individual dragons you buy are in good shape. There are a few things you should look for in checking out Chinese Water Dragons before you buy. The more time you spend making this decision, the more likely you are to bring home a healthy dragon.

Some of the most important things to look for in a healthy Chinese Water Dragon include good size and a lack of visible deformities. It is always a good idea to purchase baby or juvenile Chinese Water Dragons rather than adults, especially if they are wild-caught. Ideally, the dragon should be between 10 and 16 inches (25 to 40 cm) long. In terms of physical deformities, you should check the dragon for signs of infection. Look for patches of discolored skin, swelling, bruises or cuts. You may also want to look around the lizard's cage to check for signs of diarrhea because that may point to an internal problem.

Do not be tempted to purchase a Chinese Water Dragon that is not completely healthy under the idea that you will nurse it back to health. If the dragon is already sick, the chances are good that it will only get sicker once you take it home. Your best bet is to start out with a young, healthy dragon that you can tame and enjoy as it grows. If you plan to keep multiple Chinese Water Dragons, you might want to consider buying them all at the same time so you do not have problems down the line when introducing new dragons to the enclosure.

Guidelines for Selecting a Healthy Dragon

- Avoid adult dragons that have been imported from the wild. Imported dragons are often in poor condition and may not adapt as well as younger animals. Adults that have been captive-raised can be kept as pets.

- If you plan to purchase wild-caught dragons, it is best to purchase juvenile dragons between 10 and 16 inches (25 to 40 cm) in length – these dragons adapt well to captivity.
- If a juvenile dragon is unavailable, a wild-caught hatchling is a good second choice. The mortality rate for hatchlings may be higher than for captive-raised adults.
- Check the dragon's eyes before buying – they should be bright and clear. The body and tail should be rounded.
- If possible, handle the animal prior to purchase – examine the body for areas of swelling, lumps or skin damage. Check to be sure the limbs and tail are not injured.
- Gently tap the dragon's snout to get it to open its mouth – check to be sure the teeth are healthy and there are no signs of swelling in the mouth.

Chapter Six: Caring for Chinese Water Dragons

1.) Habitat Requirements

If you want to keep your Chinese Water Dragons happy, you need to provide them with a healthy living space. A cage for these lizards needs to be fairly large and it should provide both terrestrial and aquatic areas. It is important to remember that your Chinese Water Dragons can grow up to 36 inches long - 24 inches for females (91 or 61 cm), so you need to provide as much space as possible. Rather than purchasing another cage as your dragon grows, start off with the largest cage you can.

The minimum recommended tank size for Chinese Water

Dragons is 75 gallons (284 liters), though more is definitely better. If you plan to keep multiple dragons, you should plan to invest in a cage that measures at least four feet long and five to six feet tall. You should provide your dragons with plenty of limbs and branches to climb in as well as a tank or tub of water to soak and swim in. It is also important that you keep the cage sufficiently humid for your dragons so it accurately replicates the natural environment of these creatures.

a.) Choosing or Building a Cage

You have two options when it comes to choosing a Chinese Water Dragon enclosure – you can purchase a fabricated tank or you can build one yourself. The benefit of purchasing a fabricated tank is that it may already be assembled and it may come with a lid and other fixtures for attaching lights and heating implements. In building your own tank, however, you have the opportunity to customize the cage to accommodate your preferred setup.

If you choose to build your own cage, you need to be careful about choosing a material that will not harm your dragons. Wire or mesh cages will give your dragons something to climb on, but they can also cause skin or snout damage. The most commonly used cage material is glass, particularly Plexiglas. In using glass as a building material for your cage, it is important that you decorate the cage in such a way that prevents your dragons from bumping their snouts against the walls. The easiest way to do so is to line the borders of the cage with live or artificial plants.

Another popular option in building material for Chinese Water Dragon cages is wood. Wood will help to insulate your enclosure naturally, helping it to retain heat. In cold areas, a cage made of wood on two or three sides will be much more efficient in retaining heat than an all-glass cage. When using wood as a building material it is important to use non-toxic materials. You may also need to coat the wood with polyurethane to waterproof it.

b.) Cage Location

The location you choose for your Chinese Water Dragon cage is very important. The four most important factors to consider are:

- Visibility
- Accessibility
- Lighting
- Safety

Visibility – The whole point of keeping Chinese Water Dragons as pets is to enjoy them so you should choose a cage location that allows you to easily view your dragons. Don't keep your dragons in a back room but don't put them somewhere where their cage will be in the way.

Accessibility – Another important factor to consider is how easily accessible the cage is. When it comes to feeding your dragons and maintaining their tank, you should be able to easily access the cage.

Lighting – Chinese Water Dragons require a warm, humid environment so placing the cage near a source of natural light may help to keep the temperature up in the cage.

Safety – The safety of your Chinese Water Dragons should be very important to you. When choosing a cage location, pick a place where the opening of the cage will not be easily accessible by children or other pets. You should also avoid placing the cage in a location where people might run into it or hit it with something.

c.) Decorating the Enclosure

When it comes to decorating a Chinese Water Dragon cage you have many options to choose from but it is important that you do not go overboard. Live plants are an excellent option because they enhance the aesthetics of your tank while also providing things for your dragons to climb. Living plants can also help maintain the humidity of the enclosure, making it a more suitable environment for your dragons.

If you choose to use live plants in your dragon enclosure you should be careful to pick species that are non-toxic to reptiles. Ask the associates at your local pet store about which of their live plant selection are safe for reptiles. If you are nervous, you can always stick with the option of artificial plants. Fake plants are easy to clean but will still provide your dragons with things to climb on.

In addition to adding foliage to your dragon enclosure, you should also be sure to provide a basking area. Chinese Water Dragons require a basking area that reaches about 90°F (32°C) – this can be accomplished by setting up a heat lamp over a flat rock. Your dragons may also appreciate the inclusion of rock caves in their enclosure to provide them with a place to rest and hide.

d.) Tips for Housing Multiple Dragons

Chinese Water Dragons are generally very friendly as pets but they do require a certain degree of care. If you plan to keep multiple dragons, you need to carefully plan it out. Male dragons have a tendency to become aggressive so it is unwise to keep multiple males in the same enclosure. If you do, the dragons may fight which could result in serious injury or death of one or both dragons. It may be possible to keep two males in one cage if they have been raised together, but you should observe them during short sessions of cohabitation, watching for signs of aggression.

Your best bet for keeping multiple Chinese Water Dragons is to keep one male and several females. This is especially important if you plan to breed your dragons. If you don't plan to breed your dragons, two female dragons can generally coexist peacefully in one cage. As is true of housing multiple male dragons together, it is always a good idea to supervise the introduction of new dragons to ensure that they do not fight.

Summary of Habitat Requirements

Minimum Size: 75-gallon tank (284 liters)
Ideal Size: bigger is better; it is best to start off with a bigger tank rather than upgrading as your dragon grows
Material: glass or Plexiglas preferred; wood is a good alternative; avoid wire or mesh walls
Location: consider visibility, accessibility, lighting and safety in choosing a location
Decorations: live or artificial plants for climbing; rock caves to provide hiding places; logs or branches
Tank Temperature: 75° to 85°F (24° - 29°C)
Basking Temperature: 90°F (32°C)
Lighting: UVB lamp for basking

Water: provide a tub or pan of water for soaking and swimming

Other Notes: tank should be moist and humid

2.) Heating and Lighting

One of the most important aspects of creating a healthy environment for your Chinese Water Dragons is to maintain proper heating and lighting. The recommended daytime temperature for these lizards is around 80°F (27°C) with nighttime temperatures not dropping below 75°F (24°C). Your dragons will also require basking sites averaging 90°F (32°C) in order to keep their body temperatures within the desired range.

a.) Temperature Maintenance Tips

To achieve the ideal temperature in your Chinese Water Dragon's tank, you may want to consider investing in a reflector-type light fixture with an incandescent spotlight. These fixtures can be positioned above your dragon's tank, the spotlight positioned so that it illuminates about 40% of the tank. You can also consider installing reptile heating pads on the underside of your dragon's tank to keep the substrate warm – this will keep the temperature in the tank from falling too low at night.

In order to maintain the desired heating and lighting levels in your tank, it is a good idea to connect your equipment to a thermostat or an automatic timer. Thermostats can be programed to shut off heating devices once the tank reaches a certain temperature – this can prevent the enclosure from overheating. An automatic timer, on the other hand, is useful for tank lighting because it will regulate the daytime/nighttime cycle for your lizards. Ideally, your dragons should get 8 to 12 hours of daylight and 8 to 12 hours of nighttime. This means that you should turn off the lights in your tank at night or install an automatic timer to shut them off automatically.

b.) Tips for Creating Basking Areas

Baking areas are a necessity in creating the ideal Chinese Water Dragon enclosure because they provide space for your dragons to bask and also give them a place to hide. If your dragons are stressed, they may seek out hiding places or they might simply enjoy the heat of a basking area in the cage. Basking areas should be maintained at a temperature around 90°F (32°C) and it is a good idea to hide the basking area among live plants or artificial foliage to make your dragons feel more secure.

To heat the basking area, set up a UVB lamp directly over the area. The lamp should be positioned approximately 10 inches (25 cm) above the basking surface with no glass or plastic obstructing the heat. By placing a flat rock or piece of wood beneath the lamp, you can provide your dragons with a comfortable basking surface. If you plan to keep multiple dragons in the enclosure, be sure to provide several basking areas so each dragon can have its own.

c.) The Importance of UVB Lighting

All reptiles require certain levels of Vitamin D3 in order to be healthy. If your dragons don't receive adequate levels of Vitamin D3, their bodies may not be able to absorb calcium. If your dragons don't get any exposure to natural sunlight, you should consider installing a UVB lamp in their tank. If you are able to provide your dragons with natural sunlight, aim for between four and eight hours of exposure per week. The best time for sun exposure is between the hours of 10 a.m. and 3 p.m.

d.) Maintaining Humidity Levels

In addition to heating and lighting for your Chinese Water Dragon Tank, you also need to maintain the right humidity. The ideal humidity level for these lizards is between 70%

and 80%. To achieve this, all you have to do is provide a large container of water (which can also be used for soaking) heated by one or more spotlights. The evaporation of the water will help to raise the humidity in the tank. The addition of damp substrate and live plants in the tank will also help maintain humidity.

3.) Feeding Requirements

Chinese Water Dragons are omnivorous by nature, but they generally prefer meat over vegetables. The majority of a their diet should be composed of insects including crickets, wax worms, butter worms and silkworms – pinkie mice can also be offered, but only one to two times per week. It is important to maintain variety in your Chinese Water Dragon's diet because these animals tend to get bored with a bland diet and may end up refusing to eat.

These lizards enjoy having a different meal each day, so you may need to come up with some kind of feeding schedule to accommodate this preference. Be sure to keep a wide variety of feeder insects on hand in addition to various fruits and vegetables. Most Chinese Water Dragons are not terribly fond of fruits and vegetables and these foods should only account for 10% to 15% of your dragon's daily diet. Some good fruits and veggies to keep on hand include blueberries, raspberries, cantaloupe, figs, collard greens, sweet potato, carrots and green beans. You will also need to provide your dragon with access to fresh, clean water to drink.

a.) Types of Food

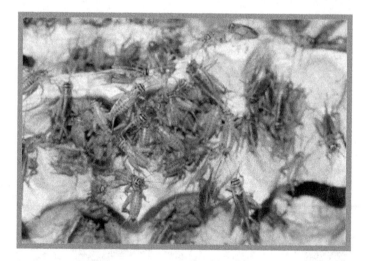

Chinese Water Dragons enjoy a variety of foods but only certain kinds are recommended. The following foods are safe for Chinese Water Dragons:

Insects:

- Crickets
- Wax worms
- Earthworms
- Butter worms
- Silk worms
- Mealworms
- Grasshoppers
- Locusts

Produce:

- Blueberries
- Raspberries
- Cantaloupe
- Figs
- Collard greens
- Sweet potato
- Carrots
- Green beans

Other:

- Small feeder fish
- Pinkie mice (newborn mice)
- Fuzzies (juvenile mice)

b.) Buying Food and Feeding Guide

There are several ways to go about getting food for your dragons. The simplest option is to simply stop by your local pet store and pick up some fresh crickets or mealworms.

You may also be able to find other worms as well as feeder fish and pinkie mice at your local pet store. Another option is to order your dragon's food online – this is a very convenient and often cost-effective method. A final option is to raise the insects yourself at home.

The amount of food you offer your Chinese Water Dragons will vary depending on their size. The easiest answer to this question is: as much as your dragons will eat. Different dragons will have different appetites so it is a good idea to keep a record of your feedings so you know how much your dragons are likely to eat. This will help you plan your meals and will also help you to notice immediately if your dragon loses his appetite. A healthy adult Chinese Water Dragon should consume at least a dozen crickets and upwards of 30 worms plus a pinkie mouse on a weekly basis.

c.) Designing a Feeding Schedule

A feeding schedule for Chinese Water Dragons largely depends on the animal's age. Juvenile dragons need to be fed more frequently than adults to promote healthy growth. While adults only need to be fed every two to three days, juveniles require daily feeding. You may choose to feed your adult dragon every day, just be sure to keep the portion sizes for those daily meals fairly small to prevent your dragon from gaining excess weight.

To make your life easier, try to draw up a feeding schedule so you can accommodate your dragon's preference for meal variety. Keep a number of different feeder insects on hand and offer a different kind of insect at each feeding. In addition to insects, you can also offer your dragons small portions of chopped vegetables or fruits, but these foods should not compose the majority of your dragon's diet. Remember that small food particles are easier for your dragon to digest than large ones.

d.) Supplementing Your Dragon's Diet

Though offering your dragon a well-balanced diet should provide adequate nutrition, your dragon may benefit from occasional supplementation. The most common supplement used for Chinese Water Dragons is calcium – you can find calcium in powder form which can be dusted over your dragon's food. Calcium is an incredibly important part of your dragon's nutrition because, if they do not receive enough, they could develop metabolic bone disease. Calcium is also essential for maintaining various bodily functions including blood clotting and muscle contraction.

If you can't find reptile calcium supplements, you can purchase human-grade calcium and vitamin D supplements then crush them yourself. Be sure to grind the supplements into a fine powder and lightly dust your dragon's food every other feeding. Be sure not to over-supplement your dragon's diet with calcium because it is possible to have too much of a good thing. Extremely high levels of calcium can actually become toxic for your dragon.

e.) Feeding Precautions

In order to keep your dragons healthy, you need to make sure to offer the right types of food in the right amounts. You should also be intentional in what combination you offer the foods. As a general rule, live insects should make up about 50% of each meal for your dragons. Worms can account for about 20% of the remaining 50% and fruit and vegetables should not exceed 15% of the meal. You can also include pinkie mice or baby rats if your dragon is large enough to handle these foods.

Whole prey is a great source of protein and other nutrients for your Chinese Water Dragons but you still need to be sure to offer variety. Feeding your dragon too much of one thing may result in nutritional deficiencies whereas a varied diet is more likely to provide well-balanced nutrition. When offering your dragon insects, it is wise to "gut-load" them by feeding the insects healthy fruits and vegetables. When your dragon eats the insects, he will also benefit from the nutrients the insects consumed.

Not only do you need to be mindful of what kinds of food you offer your Chinese Water Dragon, but you also need to consider where you get the food. It is generally not a good idea to feed your dragon insects that you catch in your backyard because they could contain traces of pesticides or other toxic chemicals. Your best bet is to purchase feeder insects from your local pet store or raise the insects yourself. Raising your own feeder insects is easier than you might think and it is both a cost-effective and convenient method of keeping a supply of your dragon's food on hand.

f.) Contaminated Food and Water

Internal parasite infections are often the result of contaminated food or water and they can be very serious. To avoid infections, it is important that you procure your feeder insects from a healthy source – only purchase from a pet store or pet supply company or raise the insects yourself. You should also be careful in regard to feeding your dragon fruits and vegetables. The best idea is to purchase organic produce to avoid exposing your dragon to pesticides and other toxic chemicals. You should also be sure to thoroughly rinse the produce before offering it to your dragon.

4.) Breeding Chinese Water Dragons

Breeding Chinese Water Dragons is not particularly difficult, but it is always a good idea to start by having your dragons examined by a vet to ensure they are healthy enough for breeding. Generally, Chinese Water Dragons reach sexual maturity around 2 years of age or when they reach a length around 24 inches (61 cm). Keep in mind that male dragons may grow larger than 2 feet and could require more time to become mature enough for breeding.

The breeding season of Chinese Water Dragons begins in the late winter or early spring. Prior to breeding, these reptiles typically go through a period of hibernation. To induce hibernation, reduce the temperature in your dragon's enclosure and limit the exposure to light. A hibernation period should last 2 months and it may only be necessary to feed your dragons once a week during this time. Two months is the standard for a hibernation period and your dragons should automatically go into a state of hibernation when you lower the tank temperature.

At the end of the hibernation period, you can bring the temperature and lighting in your dragon cage up to normal. You should also resume feeding your dragons on a daily basis. Within a few weeks of returning to a normal schedule, male dragons should begin to exhibit breeding behavior. To encourage breeding behavior, you may want to separate the male from the females for a week or so before re-introducing them. After a successful mating, female dragons will carry the fertilized eggs for several months before laying them.

a.) Selecting Dragons for Breeding

If you hope to achieve success in breeding your dragons, you need to take the time to select the proper specimens. Not only do your dragons need to be healthy but they also need to be sexually mature and properly conditioned for breeding. Chinese Water Dragons are difficult to sex before the age of 18 months – prior to this age there is little physical difference between male and female dragons. Once the female becomes sexually mature, she will begin to lay eggs.

Once female dragons become sexually mature, they require an extra level of care. You need to provide your female dragons with a healthy diet that offers plenty of calcium in order to keep them strong and healthy for developing and laying eggs. You also need to provide a box where your dragon will feel safe laying her eggs – if she has nowhere the lay the eggs, the female may hold the eggs for too long and could become egg bound.

After selecting your male and female dragons for breeding, it is a good idea to separate them. This will keep the male from becoming too aggressive and injuring the female – it will also help to encourage breeding behavior once the dragons are re-introduced into the same cage. During the breeding process, the male dragon typically grasps the female by the head, twisting her body to achieve the ideal mating position. This process can last for up to twenty minutes and it is a good idea to separate the sexes after mating to give the female an opportunity to recover.

b.) Building an Egg Incubator

After your dragons have successfully mated and the female has laid fertile eggs, you might need to remove them from the cage and incubate them yourself. Take a small container and line the bottom with damp perlite. Next, add a layer of vermiculite and top it off with some damp peat moss. Once the container is prepared, bury the eggs and cover them with additional peat moss. You can then place the container inside an incubator.

To build an incubator, you can use a standard beverage cooler. Fill a 3- or 4-foot cooler with about 4 inches (10 cm) of water and place a brick in the center to keep the egg containers out of the water. Insert a submersible aquarium heater into the water and set it for a temperature between 84° and 86°F (29° - 30°C).

You may also want to put a thermometer in the water to monitor the temperature. The eggs should hatch after about 60 days, at which point you should house the hatchlings in a separate enclosure from the adults. It is safe to separate the hatchlings from their parents immediately after they have hatched because the parents will not provide any care for the hatchlings.

Breeding Summary

Sexual Maturity: 18 to 24 months
Mating Patterns: ideally 1 male with 2 to 3 females
Preparation for Breeding: 2 months hibernation (decreased tank temperature and lighting)

Encouraging Breeding: separate the sexes for two to three weeks following hibernation before reuniting them

Female Dragons: require a laying box; may become egg bound if one is not provided

Caring for Eggs: should be kept in an incubator (you can build one yourself)

Incubation Period: about 60 days

Other Tips: separate the sexes after breeding to give the female time to rest and recover

Separating the Hatchlings: it is safe to separate the hatchlings from their parents immediately after they have hatched because the parents won't provide any parental care for the baby dragons

Chapter Seven: Chinese Water Dragon Care Sheet

Basic Information:

Scientific Name: *Physignatus cocincinus*
Habitat: East and Southeast Asia
Size: up to 3 feet (1 meter) - females average 2 feet
Coloration: light to dark green; banding on tail; bright color on throat; light on underside
Build: tail composes 70% of body length; legs are muscular for climbing and swimming; 5 toes with sharp claws; head is triangular in shape; crest or horns on head, neck and tail
Lifespan: average 10 to 15 years
Diet: omnivorous but prefer live foods

Foods: crickets, wax worms, butter worms, silkworms, pinkie mice

Fruit and Vegetables: no more than 15% daily diet; collard greens, sweet potato, carrots, green beans, raspberries, blueberries, cantaloupe, figs

Feeding Tips: adults only need to be fed about three times a week; juveniles should be fed small meals daily

Supplements: powdered calcium recommended

Tank Set-Up Guide:

Minimum Size: 75-gallon tank (284 liters)

Material: glass or Plexiglas preferred; wood is a good alternative; avoid wire or mesh walls

Decorations: live or artificial plants for climbing; rock caves to provide hiding places; logs or branches

Basking Temperature: 90°F (32°C)

Tank Temperature: 75° to 85°F (24° to 29°C)

Breeding Tips

Sexual Maturity: 18 to 24 months

Mating Patterns: ideally 1 male with 2 to 3 females

Preparation for Breeding: 2 months hibernation (decreased tank temperature and lighting)

Caring for Eggs: should be kept in an incubator

Incubation Period: about 60 days

Chapter Eight: Keeping Your Water Dragons Healthy

1.) Common Health Problems

Like all pets, Chinese Water Dragons are prone to developing certain diseases. Keeping the cage clean and offering your dragons a healthy diet will help reduce the chances of them getting sick, but it is impossible to completely prevent disease. To ensure the greatest chance of recovery, it is best to familiarize yourself with some of the most common health problems affecting Chinese Water Dragons. If you are familiar with the signs and symptoms of disease, you will be able to react quickly and provide your dragons with the treatment they need.

The following diseases are fairly common in captive Chinese Water Dragons:

Mouth Rot

Mouth rot is one of the most common health problems affecting these lizards – this disease is also known by the name stomatitis. This condition is typically the result of a secondary infection and it affects the mouth, gums and palate of captive dragons. If the infection isn't treated properly, it can enter your dragon's bloodstream and cause your dragon's body to go septic – this condition can be fatal.

Mouth rot can develop following injury or trauma to the face and it generally presents in the form of curd-like substances growing around the mouth. Severe infections can spread internally, causing bone and/or tissue damage. To treat mouth rot, it is essential that you clean the affected area on a daily basis. You may also want to swab the area with diluted Nolvasan or Betadine. It never hurts to have your dragon examined by a veterinarian, just in case the infection is more severe than you realize.

Cause: *secondary infection as a result of injury or trauma to the face and mouth*

Symptoms: *swelling around the mouth, pus, white curd-like formations around the affected site*

Treatment: *cleaning the area daily and applying diluted Nolvasan or Betadine*

Metabolic Bone Disease

Also known as MBD, metabolic bone disease is a very serious disease, often fatal for Chinese Water Dragons. This disease is caused by a lack of calcium in the diet or insufficient exposure to UVB light. If this disease is allowed to progress untreated, it can result in muscle spasms, fractured bones and bone deformities. Other symptoms may include twitching, bumps on the legs and back or lethargy.

The best prevention and treatment for this condition is to supplement your dragon's diet with calcium. To do so, dust your dragon's food with calcium carbonate powder – you can also use a liquid supplement like calcium glubanate. Installing a UVB light in your dragon's cage can also help – as can exposure to real sunlight.

Be careful about giving your dragons too much calcium because an overdose can be harmful. Only dust your dragon's food with calcium powder every other feeding and don't exceed 2 to 3 drops of liquid calcium on a weekly basis.

Cause: *lack of calcium in the diet or insufficient exposure to UVB light*

Symptoms: *twitching, lethargy, fractured bones, muscle spasms, bumps on the legs or back*

Treatment: *supplementation with calcium carbonate powder or liquid calcium; exposure to natural sunlight or UVB light*

Respiratory Illness

Respiratory infections and illnesses are fairly common among captive Chinese Water Dragons and they are typically the result of poorly maintained enclosures. If the heat and humidity in your dragon's cage is not maintained at the proper levels, your dragon is more likely to contract some kind of respiratory infection. Symptoms of respiratory infections include mouth gaping, wheezing, heavy breathing, lethargy, decreased appetite and swollen limbs.

To prevent respiratory infections, keep your Chinese Water Dragon's cage between 84° and 88°F (28° - 31°C) with a basking area around 90°F (32°C). The cage should not get any colder than 70°F (21°C) at night. If you suspect that your dragon is beginning to develop a respiratory infection, try raising the temperature in his cage a few degrees. If he doesn't show signs of improvement, take your dragon to the vet because he may need antibiotics to recover from the infection.

Cause: *improper heat or humidity in the cage*

Symptoms: *mouth gaping, wheezing, heavy breathing, lethargy, loss of appetite, swollen limbs*

Treatment: *slight increase in cage temperature; veterinary exam to prescribe antibiotics may be necessary*

Parasite Infections

In the wild, parasites are not uncommon among Chinese Water Dragon populations. In captivity, however, parasites tend to prey on Chinese Water Dragons when they are stressed – the parasites may multiply beyond the capability of the dragon's body to handle. Parasites can affect a

Chinese Water Dragon in several different ways and the only way to tell what kind of parasites your dragon has is to take him to the vet for a fecal exam.

Common symptoms of parasites in Chinese Water Dragons include lethargy, loose stools, decreased appetite, dull eyes, failure to gain weight and worms in the stool. If not properly treated, parasite infections can become very severe and may result in the death of your dragon. If you suspect your dragon is suffering from a parasite infection, take him to the vet quickly to see if deworming or parasite medications may be needed. After treating your dragon for the infection it is essential that you thoroughly clean the cage to prevent re-infection.

Cause: *parasites multiplying, preying on dragons when they are stressed*

Symptoms: *lethargy, loose stools, decreased appetite, dull eyes, failure to gain weight and worms in the stool*

Treatment: *fecal exam to diagnose; treatment with deworming or parasite medication followed by thorough cleaning of the cage*

Skin Infections

These infections may be caused by either fungus or bacteria and they are generally a result of poorly maintained cages. If the humidity in your Chinese Water Dragon cage gets too high, it may lead to excess growth of bacteria or fungus. Many Chinese Water Dragon owners mist their cages on a regular basis but it is important to dry out the cage between mistings and to ensure proper ventilation to prevent the growth and spread of fungus.

Bacterial and fungal infections in Chinese Water Dragons most commonly appear as dark-colored patches on the skin which may be raised or filled with fluid. It is important that you take your dragon to the vet if you suspect a skin infection because your vet will need to prescribe the proper medication. Common treatments for skin infections include Nolvasan or diluted Betadine as well as bacterial or fungal creams. It is important to treat skin infections promptly because they can spread to your dragon's bloodstream and become fatal.

Cause: *fungal or bacterial growths; excess humidity or moisture in the cage*

Symptoms: *appearance of dark-colored patches on the skin which may be raised or filled with fluid*

Treatment: *Nolvasan or diluted Betadine; your vet may prescribe other fungal or bacterial creams*

Dystocia

Also known as egg binding, dystocia occurs when a female dragon is unable to lay her eggs. Even if a female dragon hasn't mated with a male, she will still lay eggs – they will, however, be unfertilized and will not develop. Egg binding is a life-threatening condition in which the female is unable to pass the eggs. It is essential that you seek treatment for this condition immediately. Even if you do get your dragon treatment, the condition can still be fatal.

Common signs of dystocia include lethargy or weakness and frenzied digging around the cage. To prevent problems with egg binding it is important that you provide your dragon with a large enough laying box and that you set it up early enough for your dragon to use it. If you don't set up the box early enough, your dragon may become egg bound and could die as a result.

Cause: *inability of a female dragon to pass eggs*

Symptoms: *lethargy or weakness, frenzied digging*

Treatment: *seek veterinary care immediately; set up a large enough laying box for your dragon before she needs it*

2.) Diagnosing and Treating Illness

It may not always be obvious when your Chinese Water Dragon is sick, so it is important to keep a close eye on him for signs of disease. The earlier you are able to diagnose a disease and start treatment, the more likely your dragon is to make a full recovery. In addition to keeping an eye on your Chinese Water Dragon, it is also a good idea to have routine check-ups with your local veterinarian to make sure he is in good condition.

There are a number of ways in which your Chinese Water Dragon may come into contact with disease. Parasites and bacteria can spread quickly in a poorly maintained cage and they can also be passed through infected food or stool. Improper heating and ventilation of your dragon's cage can also lead to health problems, namely respiratory infections. Keeping your dragon's cage clean will minimize his chances of contracting disease.

Some common signs of illness include loss of appetite, change in stool and physical changes in skin or body. If your dragon suddenly begins to lose weight or if his stool becomes runny or bloody, it is most likely the result of a parasite infection. Coughing and fluid draining from the dragon's nose or mouth are common indications of respiratory infections and skin infections typically present in the form of discolored or raised patches of skin.

If you notice that your dragon's snout is swollen, it is not necessarily a cause for alarm. Swelling in the snout is fairly common among Chinese Water Dragons that regularly bump their noses against the walls of their enclosure. This is particularly common in cages that are too small or overcrowded with decorations. If your dragon exhibits swelling or difficulty moving any of its limbs, however, you should seek veterinary care as soon as possible because it may be an indication of a serious injury or a medical condition like metabolic bone disease.

It is wise to keep the contact information for several

veterinarians in your area that treat reptiles. In the event that your regular veterinarian is out of the office, it is a good idea to have a back-up in cases of emergency. You should also contact your local emergency animal hospital to see if they treat reptiles.

3.) Shedding in Chinese Water Dragons

It is completely normal for reptiles including Chinese Water Dragons to shed and they do so on a regular basis. As your dragon grows, old skin will be shed. This process occurs more frequently in young lizards but adult dragons do still shed. Shedding can take up to two weeks and it generally begins near the head and front legs, progressing toward the upper and lower body, ending with the tail.

If your Chinese Water Dragon cage is properly maintained (particularly in regard to humidity) your dragon shouldn't have any trouble shedding. If your dragon's new skin doesn't look clean or if you notice patches of old skin retained in parts of the body, it may be a cause for concern. Not only can improper shedding be a sign of problems with cage maintenance, but it could also be an indication of systemic disease.

As your dragon begins the shedding process, his skin may begin to darken and he may spend more time in the water to loosen the old skin. It is important that you never try to "help" your dragon shed his skin by pulling on it. You can, however, slightly increase the humidity in the cage or soak your dragon in warm water for 20 minutes a day. If you are concerned with your dragon's improper shedding, seek veterinary care to diagnose and treat the problem.

4.) Taking Your Dragon to the Vet

Like all pets, Chinese Water Dragons are prone to falling ill at some point throughout their lives. In case they do, it is a good idea to have the number for a veterinarian who treats reptiles on hand. You may also want to consider taking your dragons in to the vet for routine check-ups.

Think about these things before taking your dragon to see the vet:

- The cost of veterinary exams can be more than the cost of the dragon itself.

- Many veterinarians do not treat exotic pets so it may be hard to find one in your area who does.

- The cost of treatment for your dragons could be very high and it may not be effective anyway.

- Sick dragons, particularly hatchlings and juveniles, that look like they are close to death often die with or without veterinary care.

- Adult dragons, on the other hand, often respond well to treatment.

- If you do take your dragon to the vet, be sure to do so at the initial onset of symptoms – the sooner you get your dragon treatment, the more likely he is to recover.

5.) Cleaning Up After Your Chinese Water Dragons

A clean enclosure is the key to keeping your Chinese Water Dragons healthy. Even if the cage looks clean, it may still contain harmful bacteria that could make your dragon sick.

To prevent this from happening, follow these tips for cleaning your dragon's cage on a regular basis:

- Remove dead foliage of plants on a daily basis

- Remove uneaten portions of food or treats after an hour in the cage

- Brush the tank daily if you are using live plants or potting soil as a substrate

- Remove dead crickets and leftover fruits/veggies sooner rather than later

- Use caution when offering your dragons live prey because rodents can carry infections and harmful bacteria

- Change the water in the cage multiple times daily in case your dragons urinate or defecate in it

- Disinfect water and food bowls regularly

The frequency with which your dragon defecates may vary according to a number of factors. Some dragons may defecate only once a day while others may do so twice or more. If you feed your dragons only a few times a week, they may defecate even less frequently. Just remember that every dragon is different -- you may want to keep a journal to record your dragon's bowel movements so you get a feel for what is "healthy" for your individual dragon. To remove solid waste from the substrate in your dragon's tank you can simply pick it up in a piece of paper towel or use a slotted scoop.

Chapter Nine: Common Mistakes Owners Make

Caring for Chinese Water Dragons can be an incredibly rewarding experience. These reptiles are a pleasure to interact with and they can be very entertaining to watch. It is important to remember, however, that they are living creatures and not just pets. As a pet owner, it is your responsibility to care for your dragons to the best of your ability – providing for their needs and offering them a safe home.

Unfortunately, many reptile owners are unprepared for this responsibility. In this chapter you will learn about some of the most common mistakes Chinese Water Dragon owners make. Familiarizing yourself with these common mistakes will lessen your chance of repeating them yourself.

Cage Too Small

If you have ever seen Chinese Water Dragons at your local pet store, they were probably only about 5 or 6 inches (12 to 15 cm) in length – and most of that length was accounted for by the tail. Seeing these reptiles when they are small, many first-time owners do not realize how much Chinese Water Dragons grow.

An adult male dragon can grow up to 3 feet long and thus requires a great deal of space. If you start with a tank that is too small, you will need to buy a new one as your dragons grow. If you fail to provide enough space for your dragons, they will fail to thrive and could even become stressed and die as a result.

Wrong Diet

Many reptiles that are kept as pets prefer a vegetable-based diet but this is not the case with Chinese Water Dragons. Though they are omnivorous, these reptiles prefer live foods such as insects and pinkie mice. In fact, vegetables and fruit should only account for 10% to 15% of your dragon's daily diet – the rest should be composed of a variety of insects or a pinkie mouse. Another important consideration for Chinese Water Dragon diets is that these lizards can be picky eaters – if you don't provide enough variety in their diet, they could refuse to eat entirely.

Keeping Multiple Males

Chinese Water Dragons are not typically aggressive by nature but they can become territorial when they feel their home or their females are being threatened. If you keep two male dragons in the same cage, it is likely that they will begin fighting at some point – this fight could become very serious and may result in the injury or death of one of your male dragons. It can be difficult to sex Chinese Water Dragons when they are young, so ask the associates at the store where you purchase your dragons to help you make the right choice.

Combining Species

Chinese Water Dragons are very friendly pets but they do not get along with other reptile or non-reptile species. You should never, for example, house Chinese Water Dragons and geckos together. Not only could this induce stress or aggression in one or both species, but it could also be an unhealthy environment.

It is important for the health of your dragons that the tank is kept at the right temperature and humidity – other reptiles may not have the same needs in regard to tank set-up. Chinese Water Dragons may also fail to get along with other household pets like dogs or cats. In fact, the mere presence of these animals can be frightening or stressful for your dragons so, if you do have other pets, be sure to keep your dragon's tank in a safe location inaccessible to other pets.

Wrong Tank Temperature

Maintaining a stable tank temperature for your Chinese Water Dragons is incredibly important. These lizards are ectothermic creatures which means that their body heat is affected by the temperature of their environment. If the temperature in your dragon tank gets too low, it could lower your dragon's body temperature and slow down his metabolism as well as other bodily functions.

It is important to maintain a temperature between 75° and 85°F (24° to 29°C) in the tank, providing one or more basking areas heated to about 90°F (32°C). The tank should also be kept fairly humid through daily misting with fresh water.

Chapter Ten: Frequently Asked Questions

Categories of Questions Included:

General Care Concerns

Feeding Chinese Water Dragons

Breeding Chinese Water Dragons

Housing Chinese Water Dragons

Health Concerns

1.) General Care Concerns

Q: How do I know if a Chinese Water Dragon is a good choice for me?

A: Only you can make this decision but there are a number of things you should factor in before making your choice. Chinese Water Dragons live upwards of 10 years, so make sure you are ready for that kind of long-term commitment. You should also think about whether you have the space to accommodate a lizard that grows up to 3 feet long and whether you have the money to buy or build an appropriately-sized tank. If none of these things are a problem and you are interested in a friendly, entertaining reptile then a Chinese Water Dragon might be the right choice for you.

Q: What should I use to decorate my dragon's tank?

A: The goal in decorating your Chinese Water Dragon's tank is to create an environment as similar to their natural habitat as possible. Start with potting soil or peat moss as a base to maintain humidity then decorate with assorted live plants such as ficus and ferns. You can also decorate with vines and branches as well as some flat rocks or rock caves. Don't forget to include a pool of water that is large enough and deep enough for your dragon to submerge himself about halfway.

Q: Are Chinese Water Dragons hard to care for?

A: Chinese Water Dragons are not particularly difficult to care for and you don't have to have a great deal of experience or expertise with reptiles in order to do it. As long as you set up the cage properly and provide your dragons with a healthy diet you should have no trouble.

Q: Do I need to clip my dragon's claws?

A: Chinese Water Dragons have small but sharp claws. You should only have to trim your dragon's claws every two weeks or so and you should be sure to only trim the tips so it doesn't affect your dragon's climbing. To trim the nails, set your dragon on a flat surface and cut just the sharp tip of each nail with a pair of regular nail clippers.

2.) Feeding Chinese Water Dragons

Q: Does my Chinese Water Dragon need supplements?

A: If you offer your Chinese Water Dragon a healthy, well-balanced diet then he should not require supplements. Because Chinese Water Dragons are prone to developing metabolic bone disease, however, supplementing their diets with powdered calcium every other day is not a bad idea. Calcium supplementation is especially important for gravid (pregnant) females because calcium is required to form the shell on the eggs. Aside from calcium, no other supplements should be necessary.

Q: Why won't my dragon eat?

A: There are a number of possible reasons why a Chinese Water Dragon might stop eating. The most common reason is that they have grown tired of their diet. If you feed your dragons the same thing at every feeding they may become bored and could refuse to eat entirely. Another possibility is that a lack of appetite is a symptom of disease. Several diseases including sore mouth can affect your dragon's ability to eat as well as his appetite.

Q: What can I feed my dragon besides crickets?

A: Crickets are a staple of the Chinese Water Dragon's diet but it is important to offer variety. In addition to crickets, you can also offer your Chinese Water Dragon earthworms, wax worms, silkworms, small fish and even pinkie mice. You should also include a small amount of fresh fruit or vegetables in your dragon's diet, but it shouldn't compose more than 15% of his diet on any given day.

3.) Breeding Chinese Water Dragons

Q: Why is my female dragon laying eggs when I haven't even bred her?

A: Female Chinese Water Dragons will lay eggs on a regular basis, regardless whether they have been fertilized. If the eggs have been fertilized they will develop into Chinese Water Dragon hatchlings – otherwise, they will not develop at all.

Q: Why won't my dragons breed?

A: Breeding Chinese Water Dragons is not especially difficult, but there are a few things you may need to do in order to make it happen. First, your dragons need to be in optimal shape – you need to feed them a healthy well-balanced diet in order to achieve this. You may also need to induce a 2-month period of hibernation by lowering the lighting and temperature in your dragons' tank. Following the hibernation period, resume your normal feeding for a week or so before introducing the male and females back into the tank. Breeding should occur within about one week's time.

Q: When can I start breeding my Chinese Water Dragons?

A: Before you attempt to breed your Chinese Water Dragons you need to make sure they are sexually mature. These reptiles reach sexual maturity around 2 years of age or when they reach 2 feet in length. Size may vary according to sex and breeding, but Chinese Water Dragons that are 2 feet long are generally old enough to breed.

4.) Housing Chinese Water Dragons

Q: Is it okay to keep baby dragons in a large tank?

A: Yes, it is always better to provide your Chinese Water Dragons with too much space than too little. Though your dragons may only measure about 5 inches (13 cm) long when you bring them home, it will not be long before they reach a length of 2 to 3 feet. If you start off with a tank that is too small, you will have to buy or build a new one down the line when your dragons out-grow it. To save yourself the cost and hassle of doing so, start with a tank that is large enough to house your adult dragons.

Q: How should I construct my basking sites?

A: The most important aspect of a basking site is, of course, the temperature. While the general temperature in your dragon's tank should be kept between 75° and 85°F (24° to 29°C), the temperature in basking areas should be closer to 90° (32°C) or 95°F (35°C). There are a number of ways to construct a basking site but the most common is to use a

UVB lamp. Position the lamp about 10 inches (25 cm) above the basking site which, ideally, is a large flat rock that will absorb the heat. You can also use electric heating pads attached to the underside of the tank to provide warmth.

Q: What is the best material for a Chinese Water Dragon tank?

A: When it comes to choosing a building material for your Chinese Water Dragon tank there are several things you need to consider. One of the most important considerations is practicality. Chinese Water Dragons are semi-terrestrial so they require access to water -- a tank entirely composed of mesh will not be able to accommodate this preference unless you install a water tank. If you are purchasing rather than building a tank for your dragons, an all-glass or Plexiglas tank is your best bet.

Q: What steps should I take to build a Chinese Water Dragon vivarium?

A: Start by choosing a large tank to use for your vivarium and make sure it comes with a screened lid (or buy one separately). Purchase the necessary heating and lighting equipment to keep your dragon's enclosure at the ideal temperature, both day and night. Position the basking lamp so it covers about 40% of the enclosure – the temperature on the other side of the tank should be slightly cooler. Line the bottom of the tank with some kind of substrate such as coconut fiber, reptile carpet or bark bedding. Decorate the tank with live plants, branches and rocks. Be sure to provide your dragons with access to water for soaking and set the lights on a timer to provide 8 to 12 hours of light daily.

5.) Health Concerns

Q: How can I prevent my dragons from getting sick?

A: The best way to prevent illness is to keep your dragons well-fed and your cage clean. If you fail to regularly clean your dragon's tank, your dragons could be exposed to pathogenic bacteria, fungi and viruses. Providing your dragons with a well-balanced diet will help keep them healthy and strong – better able to fight off disease and infection when they are exposed.

Q: My dragon's snout looks swollen, what should I do?

A: If your Chinese Water Dragon's snout looks swollen, it is most likely because he has been bumping it into the walls or decorations in his tank. This is a common problem when Chinese Water Dragons are kept in cages that are too small. If this is not an issue, try rearranging the tank so that the walls are lined with plants or other decorations to prevent your dragon from running into them.

Q: Why is my dragon's skin discolored?

A: Discolored patches of skin are common in cases of bacterial or fungal infections. These infections are often the result of a poorly maintained tank or one that is too moist. Though Chinese Water Dragons require a humid environment, keeping the tank too moist could encourage the growth of bacteria and fungus. If you notice discolored or swollen areas on your dragon's body, take him to the vet as soon as possible for diagnosis and treatment.

Chapter Eleven: Relevant Websites

1.) Food for Chinese Water Dragons

United States Websites:

"Chinese Water Dragon Care Guide – Section 6." Herp Center Network. <http://www.herpcenter.com/reptile-caresheets/water-dragon/chinese-water-dragon-care-6.html>

"What do Chinese Water Dragons Eat?" Chinese Water Dragon Care. <http://www.chinesewaterdragon.net/chinese-water-dragons-food-feeding/>

"Chinese Water Dragon Care Guide – Section 5." Herp Center Network. <http://www.herpcenter.com/reptile-caresheets/water-dragon/chinese-water-dragon-care-5.html>

UK Websites:

"Chinese Water Dragon Caresheet." The Pet Shop U.K. <http://www.thepetshopuk.co.uk/index.php?main_page=page&id=8>

"Asian (Green/Chinese) Water Dragons." Coast to Coast Exotics. <http://www.coasttocoast.co.uk/waterdragons.html>

"The Chinese or Thai Water Dragon. "Sauria.org.uk. <http://www.sauria.org.uk/cap_breed/animals/waterdrag.htm>

2.) Care of Chinese Water Dragons

United States Websites:
"Fact Sheets." Smithsonian National Zoological Park.
<http://nationalzoo.si.edu/Animals/ReptilesAmphibians/Fac
ts/FactSheets/Asianwaterdragon.cfm>

Power, Tricia. "Care of the Chinese Water Dragon." Tricia's
Water Dragon, Reptile and Amphibian Care Page.
<http://www.triciaswaterdragon.com/dragoncr.htm>

"Chinese Water Dragon Care Information."
ReptileChannel.com. <
http://www.reptilechannel.com/lizards/lizard-
species/chinese-water-dragon-species.aspx>

UK Websites:

Banfield, Lee. "Chinese Water Dragon Care Sheet."
TheReptilian.co.uk.
<http://www.thereptilian.co.uk/care_sheets/Chinese_water_
dragon_Physignathus_cocincinus_care_sheet.htm>

Paterson, Erik. "Chinese Water Dragon Care."
ErikPaterson.co.uk.
<http://www.erikpaterson.co.uk/waterdragons.htm>

"Chinese Water Dragons as Exotic Pets – Care Sheet."
PredatorsExoticPets.co.uk.
<http://www.predatorsexoticpets.co.uk/exotic-pets-care-sheets/chinese-water-dragon-as-exotic-pets-care-sheet>

3.) Health of Chinese Water Dragons

United States Websites:

"Common Medical Conditions Affecting Chinese Water Dragons. Chinese Water Dragon Care. <http://www.chinesewaterdragon.net/health-concerns-common-medical-conditions/>

"Asian or Chinese Water Dragon – Captive Care and Common Health Concerns." HerpNation Media. <http://www.herpnation.com/hn-blog/frank-indiviglio/asian-or-chinese-water-dragon-%E2%80%93-captive-care-and-common-health-concerns/?simple_nav_category=frank-indiviglio>

Power, Tricia. "Common Ailments of Chinese Water Dragons in Captivity." Tricia's Chinese Water Dragon, Reptile and Amphibian Care Page. <http://www.triciaswaterdragon.com/ailments.htm>

UK Websites:

"Water Dragons." ExoticPetVet.co.uk. <http://www.barrieranimalcareclinic.co.uk/epv/lizards/Water%20Dragons.pdf>

Hernandez-Divers, Stephen J. "Care of the Thai Water Dragon." ACVets.co.uk. <https://www.google.com/url?sa=t&rct=j&q=&esrc=s&source=web&cd=5&cad=rja&ved=0CFAQFjAE&url=http%3A%2F%2Fwww.acvets.co.uk%2Fcaresheets%2Flizards%2FWater-Dragons.docx&ei=1jKVUY_1F8Wp4AOtvIHADA&usg=AFQjCNGrERbFCvvMuom9eZRfL78d3Td_vQ&sig2=I1UmesljFEp-elQyM3_aEA>

"Chinese Water Dragon." The Animal Zone UK. <http://www.theanimalzoneuk.com/WebRoot/BT4/Shops/BT4098/MediaGallery/Caresheets/Chinese_Water_Dragon.pdf>

4.) General Information for Chinese Water Dragons

United States Websites:

"Chinese Water Dragon Care Sheet." The Lizard Lounge. <http://www.the-lizard-lounge.com/content/species/chinese-water-dragon.asp>

"Chinese Water Dragon." Potter Park Zoo. <http://www.potterparkzoo.org/our-animals/reptiles-amphibians/chinese-water-dragon>

"Chinese Water Dragon Care Guide." Herp Center Network. <http://www.herpcenter.com/reptile-caresheets/water-dragon/>

UK Websites:

"Physignathus Cocincinus – Chinese Water Dragons." Lizards Emporium. <http://www.lizardloungeblackpool.co.uk/page/chinese_water_dragon>

"Chinese Water Dragon." TC Reptiles. <http://www.tcreptiles.co.uk/chinesewaterdragoncar.htm>

"Chinese Water Dragon Caresheet." PawsforThought.co.uk. <http://www.pawsforthought.co.uk/reptile-caresheets/chinese-water-dragon-caresheet>

Index

References

Acana, A. "Guide to Philippine Flora and Fauna." Vol X, Amphibians and Reptiles/Natural Resources Management Center. Ministry of Natural Resources and University of Philippines; Philippines, 1986.

"Asian (Green/Chinese) Water Dragons." Coast to Coast Exotics.
<http://www.coasttocoast.co.uk/waterdragons.html>

"Asian or Chinese Water Dragon – Captive Care and Common Health Concerns." HerpNation Media.
<http://www.herpnation.com/hn-blog/frank-indiviglio/asian-or-chinese-water-dragon-%E2%80%93-captive-care-and-common-health-concerns/?simple_nav_category=frank-indiviglio>

Banfield, Lee. "Chinese Water Dragon Care Sheet." TheReptilian.co.uk.
<http://www.thereptilian.co.uk/care_sheets/Chinese_water_dragon_Physignathus_cocincinus_care_sheet.htm>

"Chinese Water Dragon." Petco.com.
<http://www.petco.com/caresheets/lizards/Dragon_Chinese_Water.pdf>

"Chinese Water Dragon." Potter Park Zoo.
<http://www.potterparkzoo.org/our-animals/reptiles-amphibians/chinese-water-dragon>

"Chinese Water Dragon." The Animal Zone UK.
<http://www.theanimalzoneuk.com/WebRoot/BT4/Shops/BT4098/MediaGallery/Caresheets/Chinese_Water_Dragon.pdf>

"Chinese Water Dragon Care Guide." Herp Center
Network. <http://www.herpcenter.com/reptile-caresheets/water-dragon/>
"Chinese Water Dragon." TC Reptiles.
<http://www.tcreptiles.co.uk/chinesewaterdragoncar.htm>

"Chinese Water Dragon Care Guide – Section 5." Herp
Center Network. <http://www.herpcenter.com/reptile-caresheets/water-dragon/chinese-water-dragon-care-5.html>

"Chinese Water Dragon Care Guide – Section 6." Herp
Center Network. <http://www.herpcenter.com/reptile-caresheets/water-dragon/chinese-water-dragon-care-6.html>

"Chinese Water Dragon Care Information."
ReptileChannel.com. <
http://www.reptilechannel.com/lizards/lizard-species/chinese-water-dragon-species.aspx>

"Chinese Water Dragon Caresheet." PawsforThought.co.uk.
<http://www.pawsforthought.co.uk/reptile-caresheets/chinese-water-dragon-caresheet>

"Chinese Water Dragon Caresheet." The Pet Shop U.K.
<http://www.thepetshopuk.co.uk/index.php?main_page=page&id=8>

"Chinese Water Dragon Care Sheet." The Lizard Lounge.
<http://www.the-lizard-lounge.com/content/species/chinese-water-dragon.asp>

"Chinese Water Dragons as Exotic Pets – Care Sheet."
PredatorsExoticPets.co.uk.
<http://www.predatorsexoticpets.co.uk/exotic-pets-care-sheets/chinese-water-dragon-as-exotic-pets-care-sheet>

"Cleaning Chinese Water Dragon Enclosure." Chinese
Water Dragon Care.
<http://www.chinesewaterdragon.net/cleaning-chinese-water-dragon-enclosure/>

"Common Medical Conditions Affecting Chinese Water Dragons. Chinese Water Dragon Care. <http://www.chinesewaterdragon.net/health-concerns-common-medical-conditions/>

"Considering an Iguana as a Pet." Petco.com. <http://www.petco.com/Content/ArticleList/Article/32/6/2460/Considering-an-Iguana-as-a-Pet.aspx>

Deliz, Abby. "Caring for Chinese Water Dragons." Suite101. <http://suite101.com/article/caring-for-chinese-water-dragons-a69490>

Demeter, B.U. "Maintenance and Breeding of the Chinese Water Dragon (Physignathus cocincinus) at the National Zoological Park." 5th Annual Symposium on Captive Propogation and Husbandry; Oklahoma City Zoo, 1981.

"Fact Sheets." Smithsonian National Zoological Park. <http://nationalzoo.si.edu/Animals/ReptilesAmphibians/Facts/FactSheets/Asianwaterdragon.cfm>

Frye, F.L. "Reptile Care: Atlas of Diseases and Treatments." T.F.H. Neptune, New Jersey; 1991.

"Get Familiar with Signals Given by Sick Dragons." Chinese Water Dragon Care.

<http://www.chinesewaterdragon.net/know-signals-by-sick-dragons/>

"Getting an Animal Keeper's License to Keep Reptiles." Environment and Heritage. <http://www.environment.nsw.gov.au/wildlifelicences/GettingAReptileKeepersLicence.htm>

Hancock, Christine. "Care and Feeding of Iguanas." Avian & Exotic Animal Hospital. < http://www.drexotic.com/care-and-feeding-of-iguanas/>

Hernandez-Divers, Stephen J. "Care of the Thai Water Dragon." ACVets.co.uk. <https://www.google.com/url?sa=t&rct=j&q=&esrc=s&source=web&cd=5&cad=rja&ved=0CFAQFjAE&url=http%3A%2F%2Fwww.acvets.co.uk%2Fcaresheets%2Flizards%2FWater-Dragons.docx&ei=1jKVUY_1F8Wp4AOtvIHADA&usg=AFQjCNGrERbFCvvMuom9eZRfL78d3Td_vQ&sig2=I1UmesljFEp-elQyM3_aEA>

"Is My Water Dragon Sick?" Chinese Water Dragons. <http://chinesewaterdragons.tripod.com/id6.html>

"Is Your Chinese Water Dragon Not Shedding Normally?" Chinese Water Dragon Care. <http://www.chinesewaterdragon.net/abnormal-shedding/>

Lederer, G. "An Additional Contribution to the Ethnology of the Sail-Lizard (Hydrosaurus amboinensis Schloss). Bulletin Chicago Herpetological Society, 22 (9): Chicago, Illinois.

Mader, D.R. "captive Propagation of the Chinese Water Dragon (Physignathus concincinus)." Proceedings of the Northern California Herpetological Society's 1987 Conference on Captive Propagation and Husbandry of Reptiles and Amphibians: California, 1987.

Masters, Madeline. "Water Dragon vs. Bearded Dragon." PawNation. <http://animals.pawnation.com/water-dragon-vs-bearded-dragon-2717.html>

Michell, L.A. "Comments on the Maintenance and Reproduction of Hydrosaurus pustulatus at the Dallas Zoo." In the Proceedings of the 9th International Herpetological Symposium on Captive Propagation and Husbandry. 1985.

Paterson, Erik. "Chinese Water Dragon Care." ErikPaterson.co.uk. <http://www.erikpaterson.co.uk/waterdragons.htm>

"Physignathus Cocincinus – Chinese Water Dragons." Lizards Emporium.

<http://www.lizardloungeblackpool.co.uk/page/chinese_water_dragon>

Power, Tricia. "Care of the Chinese Water Dragon." Tricia's Water Dragon, Reptile and Amphibian Care Page. <http://www.triciaswaterdragon.com/dragoncr.htm>

Power, Tricia. "Common Ailments of Chinese Water Dragons in Captivity." Tricia's Chinese Water Dragon, Reptile and Amphibian Care Page. <http://www.triciaswaterdragon.com/ailments.htm>

"Sexing Your Chinese Water Dragon." Tricia's Chinese Water Dragon, Reptile and Amphibian Care Page. <http://www.triciaswaterdragon.com/sex.htm>

"The Chinese or Thai Water Dragon. "Sauria.org.uk. <http://www.sauria.org.uk/cap_breed/animals/waterdrag.htm>

"The Dangerous Wild Animals Act 1976." Legislation.gov.uk. <http://www.legislation.gov.uk/uksi/2007/2465/schedule/made>

"The Reptile and Amphibian Communities in the United States." Centers for Epidemiology and Animal Health.

<http://www.aphis.usda.gov/animal_health/emergingissues/downloads/reptile.pdf>

"Water Dragons." ExoticPetVet.co.uk. <http://www.barrieranimalcareclinic.co.uk/epv/lizards/Water%20Dragons.pdf>

"What do Chinese Water Dragons Eat?" Chinese Water Dragon Care. <http://www.chinesewaterdragon.net/chinese-water-dragons-food-feeding/>

Photo Credits

Title Page Photo, By Jakub Hałun (Own work) [GFDL (http://www.gnu.org/copyleft/fdl.html) via Wikimedia Commons

Page 1 Photo, By pam fray [CC-BY-SA-2.0 (http://creativecommons.org/licenses/by-sa/2.0)], via Wikimedia Commons

Page 3 Photo, By pam fray [CC-BY-SA-2.0 (http://creativecommons.org/licenses/by-sa/2.0)], via Wikimedia Commons

Page 3 Photo, By Kerstin Franke (Tinie) [GFDL (http://www.gnu.org/copyleft/fdl.html), CC-BY-SA-3.0 via Wikimedia Commons

Page 6 Photo, By Christine Matthews, licensed for reuse under Creative Commons License, <http://www.geograph.org.uk/photo/2405854>

Page 9 Photo, By inas66 (Own work) [CC-BY-SA-3.0 (http://creativecommons.org/licenses/by-sa/3.0)], via Wikimedia Commons

Page 11 Photo, By en:User:Cburnett (Own work) [GFDL (http://www.gnu.org/copyleft/fdl.html) via Wikimedia Commons

Page 13 Photo, By SeaDave from Fairlie, Scotland (Iguana Uploaded by MaybeMaybeMaybe) [CC-BY-2.0 (http://creativecommons.org/licenses/by/2.0)], via Wikimedia Commons

Page 16 Photo, By Leszek Leszczynski (Water Dragon) [CC-BY-2.0 (http://creativecommons.org/licenses/by/2.0)], via Wikimedia Commons

Page 19 Photo, By Flickr user Quinet

Page 22 Photo, By Mätes II. (Own work) [GFDL (http://www.gnu.org/copyleft/fdl.html via Wikimedia Commons

Page 24 Photo, By DeviantART user LilWy, <http://lilwy.deviantart.com/art/Hello-There-131478216>

Page 26 Photo, By Pengo (Own work) [CC-BY-SA-3.0 (http://creativecommons.org/licenses/by-sa/3.0) via Wikimedia Commons

Page 32 Photo, By Kerstin Franke (Tinie) (Own work) [CC-BY-SA-2.0-de (http://creativecommons.org/licenses/by-

sa/2.0/de/deed.en), GFDL
(http://www.gnu.org/copyleft/fdl.html) via Wikimedia
Commons

Page 33 Photo By Flickr user Nature'sAura

Page 36 Photo, By Sylfred1977 (Own work) [GFDL
(http://www.gnu.org/copyleft/fdl.html) via Wikimedia
Commons

Page 38 Photo, By Flickr user Glen Bowman

Page 41 Photo, By Camphora (Own work) [GFDL
(http://www.gnu.org/copyleft/fdl.html) via Wikimedia
Commons

Page 43 Photo, By Flickr user Mcamcamca

Page 45 Photo, By Jakub Hałun (Own work) [GFDL
(http://www.gnu.org/copyleft/fdl.html) via Wikimedia
Commons

Page 50 Photo, By Flickr user Nature'sAura

Page 53 Photo, By Flickr user David Shane

Page 54 Photo, By LEAPTOUY (Own work) [Public
domain], via Wikimedia Commons

Page 59 Photo, By Cele4, Wikimedia Commons, <http://commons.wikimedia.org/wiki/File:Wasseragame1cel e4.jpg>

Page 61 Photo, By Flickr user Debs

Page 63 Photo, By Kerstin Franke (Tinie) (Own work) [CC-BY-SA-2.0-de (http://creativecommons.org/licenses/by-sa/2.0/de/deed.en) via Wikimedia Commons

Page 65 Photo, By Kerstin Franke (Tinie) (Own work) [CC-BY-SA-2.0-de (http://creativecommons.org/licenses/by-sa/2.0/de/deed.en) via Wikimedia Commons

Page 67 Photo, 23 By Mätes II. (Own work) [GFDL (http://www.gnu.org/copyleft/fdl.html) via Wikimedia Commons

Page 69 Photo, By Emőke Dénes (Kew Gardens) [CC-BY-SA-2.5 (http://creativecommons.org/licenses/by-sa/2.5)], via Wikimedia Commons

Page 77 Photo, By Flickr user Tomi Tapio

Page 80 Photo, By Flickr user MattK1979

Page 84 Photo, By Flickr user Jim Linwood

Page 86 Photo, By Emőke Dénes (kindly granted by the author) [CC-BY-SA-2.5 (http://creativecommons.org/licenses/by-sa/2.5)], via Wikimedia Commons

Page 88 Photo By Flickr user Ben Hosking

Page 89 Photo, By Flickr user Jim Linwood,

Page 90 Photo, By frank wouters from antwerpen, belgium , België , Belgique (shining star) [CC-BY-2.0 (http://creativecommons.org/licenses/by/2.0)], via Wikimedia Commons

Page 93 Photo, By Malene Thyssen (User Malene) (Self-photographed) [GFDL (http://www.gnu.org/copyleft/fdl.html) via Wikimedia Commons

Page 104 Photo, By DenesFeri (Emőke Dénes). (Own work.) [CC-BY-SA-2.5 (http://creativecommons.org/licenses/by-sa/2.5)], via Wikimedia Commons

CPSIA information can be obtained
at www.ICGtesting.com
Printed in the USA
BVHW080538020619
549892BV00002B/158/P

9 780957 678002